le Sirene - 1

THE LUCANIANS IN

PÆSTUM

M. Cipriani
E. Greco
F. Longo
A. Pontrandolfo

FONDAZIONE PÆSTUM

Editor of the series
Emanuele Greco

Editorial organization
Ottavio Voza

Graphic project, editing and cover
Domenico Gasparri e Cristina Raiconi

Original title
I LUCANI A PÆSTUM

English translation
Federico Poole

EDITED WITH THE SHARE OF
AMMINISTRAZIONE PROVINCIALE DI SALERNO

FOREWORD

*F*or over two hundred years, Paestum has attracted cultivated tourists, both European and non-European, mainly drawn to this charming place by the imposing bulk of its three famous temples. It has taken many decades before it became widely recognized that Paestum is also a great ancient city, with its walls, its sanctuaries, its public buildings, its houses and tombs, elements without which it is impossible to reconstruct the history of a site. The temples themselves would remain mere isolated masterpieces, if they were not seen in this context. The first painted tombs, an eloquent testimony of the flourishing of the Lucanian civilization, were accidentally discovered as early as the beginning of the 19th century. It was, however, only a century and a half later that the 300 painted slabs recovered first in the excavations of Marzullo and then in those of Sestieri, but mostly in the large-scale investigations conducted by Mario Napoli from the end of the '60s, made the Paestum Museum one of the greatest galleries of the ancient world. Thanks to these images, to the grave-goods (vases, weapons, jewellery, terracottas), to the votive deposits of the sanctuaries and to the monuments of the city itself, we are now acquainted with one of the most important phases in the history not only of Paestum, but also of a large part of that region later to be called "Lucania", from the name of its inhabitants. This book introduces us to the Lucanian civilization in Paestum and in the surrounding territory through its abundant and spectacular archaeological vestiges.

Paestum. Necropolis of Andriuolo, tomb 12. East slab representing the return of the knight. 360 B.C.

Emanuele Greco
President of the Pæstum Foundation

1. POSEIDONIA-PAESTUM FROM THE FOUNDATION TO THE LUCANIAN CONQUEST

A s its title makes clear, the historical and geographical scope of this guide is limited, as it focuses on the Lucanians in Paestum, i.e. on the history of a city and of the territory immediately surrounding it, especially the Tyrrhenian coastal tract going from Salerno to northern Calabria, from approximately the middle of the 5th century (around 450 B.C.) to the Roman conquest of Paestum in 273 B.C. The period going from the foundation of the Latin colony, in 273 B.C., until its abandonment shall not be dealt with here. To help the reader gain a historical perspective, I shall begin with the foundation of the Greek city, and then turn to the description of the region

Map of Lucania and the neighbouring regions.

surrounding it. This will make it easier to appreciate the cultural processes underlying the transformation of the Greek city of Poseidonia into Lucanian Paestum.

Let me begin by saying that the final act of that transformation was a war: Paestum was conquered by the Lucanians.

Strabo, a historian and geographer who lived in the age of Augustus, is our most valuable source on this episode. He tells us that the Lucanians were people of Samnite origin, i.e. Italic populations who, after having defeated in battle the Poseidoniates and their allies, conquered their cities. In another, earlier passage, while briefly dealing with Poseidonia, Strabo alludes to the Greek origin of the city and to its falling first under Lucanian and then Roman domination.

Poseidonia and its territory.

Strabo does not say in what year the battle which resulted in Poseidonia's occupation on the part of the Lucanians was fought, but archaeological discoveries indicate that it must have taken place around 420 B.C. The same archaeological discoveries have also revealed that at least three decades earlier groups of Italics, easily recognizable by their funerary customs, had begun to infiltrate the city. The battle was hence the final outcome of a process which had begun earlier on. But it is now time to tell the story from the beginning.

It is Strabo, again (the literary sources concerning Paestum are unfortunately scarce), who informs us that the city was founded by settlers from Sybaris on a site lying 50 *stadii* (about 9 kilometers) south of the river Silaris (the present-day Sele). Lacking further historical data, we must turn to the archaeological evidence. In the

5

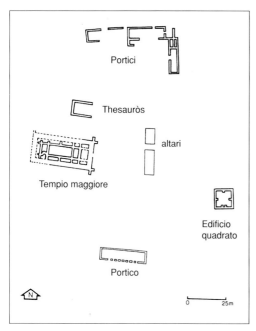

Portici

Thesauròs

Tempio maggiore

altari

Edificio
quadrato

Portico

N

0   25m

Plan of the sanctuary of Hera on the Sele.

7th century B.C., the town-area was still inhabited by indigenous populations, not especially numerous, judging from the scarce remains discovered up to now.

The first graves attributable to Greeks, instead, seem to go back to the beginning of the 6th century B.C. The first sacred buildings, both in the city and in the great sanctuary of Hera erected near the left bank of the Sele, go back to 580 ca. B.C.

Although we have very little information on the early period of this new foundation, the inhabitants of Poseidonia must have certainly appropriated the rich territory extending from the Sele to Agropoli and inland to the slopes of the part of the Alburnian chain nearest to the coast.

One of the first and most remarkable testimonies of this presence is the sanctuary of Hera (*Heraion*), which lies on the left bank of the Sele, intentionally erected in the point where the river is easiest to cross, almost as if to signal to visiting outsiders the presence of the goddess, protector of the fields, and the right of the people who inhabited them to occupy that territory.

The Paestum Museum, thanks to the systematic excavations carried out near the Sele by P. Zancani Montuoro and U. Zanotti Bianco, boasts one of the largest existing collections of Archaic Greek sculpture. The metopes,

6

Heraion on the Sele. Metope representing Artemis and Apollo shooting arrows. 560 B.C. ca.

reassembled accor-ding to the recon-struction proposed by Zancani Montuo-ro (which is currently being revised) repre-sent various mythical cycles, especially the labors of Heracles and the war of Troy, but also other sagas, such as the hero on the tortoise, the Dio-scuri chasing the Leucippides, the cy-cle of Orestes and the punishment of Sisyphus. They are datable around 560 B.C., and certainly come from at least two temple buildings. Another group of metopes, featuring a cortege of female dancers, are more recent (500 B.C.). They used to decorate the great temple of the goddess within the Sele sanctuary, where the votive offerings (vases, terracottas, jewellery), only part of which are on display in the Museum, bear witness to the abun-dance of offerings, and shed light on the peculiarities of the cult and on the types of ritual practiced in the sanc-tuary itself. Most often featured are figures of the Mother Goddess (*kourotrophos*), of the protector of child-bearers (*Ilitia*) and of the goddess with the pomegranate, a deity of the nether world.

In the city, at the time of the construction of the sanctuary on the Sele, the Poseidoniates were parceling the town area, assigning the plots for the building of sanctuaries, those for public use (in particular the agora, the main square) and those for the building of private houses.

A short time after the middle of the 6th century B.C., they began to lay out the urban grid, consisting of three great east-west streets with a width from 10 to 18 meters (for the central one) and a number of 5-meter wide streets, perpendicular to the former and placed at intervals of 35

7

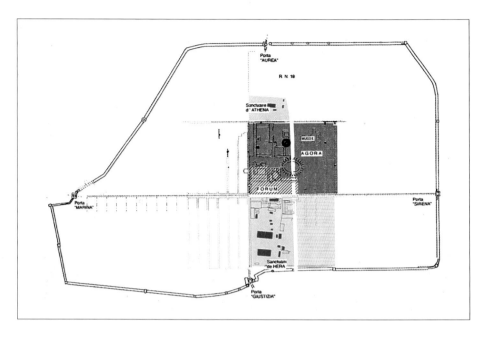

Poseidonia.
Plan of the city.

meters one from the other. The authority of Poseidonia over its regional surroundings is proved by two circumstances: in 540 B.C., the Phocaeans, who had just been defeated in Sardinian waters by an Etruscan-Carthaginian coalition, met a man from Poseidonia in *Rhegion* (present-day Reggio Calabria), who convinced them to found Velia; a few years later, around the end of the 6th century B.C., the Sybarites drew up a treaty of friendship with an Italic population called the Serdaioi (we know this from an inscription on a bronze plaque found in Olympia, in the sanctuary of the games), in which Poseidonia appears as the guarantor, evidently due to its ties with Sybaris, its mother town, but also of the credit it enjoyed among Italic populations.

We know practically nothing of the history of Poseidonia in the 5th century B.C., except that a Poseidoniate athlete named Parmenides won the competition of the stadium (a race of about 200 meters) in the 78th Olympic (468 B.C.). Between 530 and 470-60 B.C. the great architectural programs were carried out. In the area of the southern sanctuary, the temple of Hera (conventionally known as the Basilica) was the first to be erected.

It features nine columns on the facade and eighteen on the long sides. Its cell is divided in two by a central row of columns (a possible indication of the presence of two deities) preceded by two symmetrical rooms, the pronaos and the opisthodomos, respectively placed on the east and west side of the facade.

The upper parts, which were mostly made out of wood, are lost, but a remarkable series of architectural terracottas (cornices and lion-head gutters) painted in bright colors have been preserved.

In the years around 500 B.C., while the major temple on the Sele was being built, the temple of Athena (the so-called

Poseidonia.
Aerial view
of the central
zone from the south.

Temple of Ceres) was being erected in the northernmost part of the city. This *Athenaion* is a real jewel of late-Archaic Greek architecture. It presents 6 columns on its facade and 13 on its long sides, all Doric, while the cell was preceded by a spacious vestibule bordered by columns with Ionian capitals (two of which are on exhibit in the Museum). The coffered

9

decoration of the oblique cornices of the fronton and the absence of a horizontal cornice are quite unusual features. In the area of the sanctuary of Athena, south of the temple, are the foundations of an Archaic temple datable to 580 *ca.* B.C., the most ancient Paestan sacred building known to date. Its reassembled gutters are on display in the Museum.

Poseidonia. Northern
urban sanctuary.
Detail of the cornice
of the western fronton
of the so-called
temple of Ceres
(temple of Athena).
500 B.C. ca.

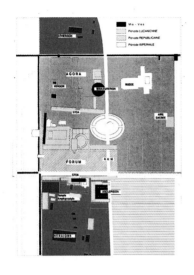

*Poseidonia. Plan
of the central zone
(including the agorá
and the sanctuaries).*

*Poseidonia.
Cenotaph.
520-510 B.C.*

Immediately south of the small hill on which the *Athenaion* is built is Poseidonia's great agora. Its extension and spatial organization are no longer clearly perceivable as, after the Roman conquest, the political and administrative center was moved further south, to the newly created forum, and the area of the old agora was reused first for private housing and later on, during the Early Middle Ages, as a cemetery. Several systematic investigations conducted in the last twenty years by a French-Italian joint mission have shed light on certain aspects of the general topography of the agora: first of all its limits, marked by four streets, two running east-west, the other two north-south, delimiting a rectangle of about 330 x 300 meters, i.e. about 10 hectares, an unusually vast area for a Greek agora, but not uncommon among Great Greek cities.

Within this great space, the monuments identified are few, although important. They go back to the time in which the area had a public function, i.e. the period between the foundation of the city and the Roman conquest.

On the east side is the *heroon* (the so-called hypogeal *sacellum*), which was discovered and excavated by Sestieri in 1954. It consists of a rectangular pit dug into the rock

bank on three sides (the fourth, to the east, has a facade built of travertine blocks) with a roof made of rock-slabs over which lies a second roof, made of large tiles. Inside, at the center of the room, two adjoining blocks formed a rock table where five iron spits lay, which had been used to roast the meat for a sacrifice. Around the table were eight bronze vases originally containing honey, very refined products, possibly made by Sybarite craftsmen, and an Attic vase (made in Athens) bearing a representation of Heracles' apotheosis, i.e. of the hero entering the Olympus accompanied by Athena.

All the objects were deposed around 520-10 B.C. The building itself must hence date to the same period. It was probably covered by a tumulus. The ensemble was certainly used for an heroic cult, of the kind that Greek cities granted to persons who were worshipped as heroes after their death for the merits they had acquired during their lifetime. Among these persons, the most important was the hero who had founded the city itself, whose monument, a cenotaph (i.e. an empty tomb) was placed in the agora, the center of political life and hence the ideal site for a cult so charged with political significance.

The Poseidonian *heroon* is presently surrounded by an enclosure made of large rock slabs. This is not its original arrangement, but a modification of the Roman period, when the tumulus was demolished and the cenotaph was surrounded with a rectangular enclosure, a token of the respect it commanded even at this late date, and the cause of its exceptional state of preservation.

On the opposite side of the square, toward the east, is Poseidonia's *ekklesiasterion*. This circular building was

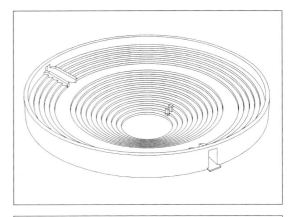

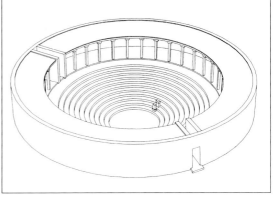

Poseidonia. Hypothetical reconstructions of the ekklesiasterion. 480-470 B.C.

11

made by excavating the rock bank in concentric circles, thus creating a series of steps on which the popular assembly, the *ekklesia*, sat during its meetings (the name *"ekklesiasterion"* means "the place where the *ekklesia* meets"). Stratigraphic evidence dates this construction to ca. 480-70 B.C. It is thus a primary source for the history of the institutions of Greek Poseidonia, which suffers from a lack of written documents. As analogous buildings were discovered in Agrigentum and Metapontum, the circular *ekklesiasterion* can be regarded as one of the most characteristic monuments of the Greeks' western experience.

Finally, on the southern side of the square, near the amphitheater, lies a great portico erected in the 4th century B.C., which I shall deal with more in detail further on, as it is a testimony of the public building activity of the city during the Lucanian domination.

In the same years in which the *ekklesiasterion* was built, the Poseidoniates had undertaken their most ambitious building project: the construction of the largest of their temples, the one which we conventionally call the "Temple of Neptune".

It is a grandiose Doric periptery, with 6 columns on its facade and 14 on its long sides, with a cell delimited by the symmetrical pronaos and opisthodomos, and divided into three naves by a double row of columns.

Apart from the frontons, no elements of the roof remain, but the excellent state of preservation and great refinement of the individual architectural elements of the temple make it one of the marvels of Doric architecture in the West at the time of its climax, shortly before the middle of the 4th century B.C.

Traditionally, this temple, erected a very short time after the Basilica, was also attributed to Hera, almost as if it was a duplicate of the other temple. Other hypotheses have been recently put forward. It has been suggested that it could be a temple of Zeus, because of its close affinities with the temple of this god in Olympia or, as Torelli has convincingly argued, a temple of Apollo.

Our survey of the Greek city wouldn't be complete without the sanctuary of S. Venera and the necropolises.

The sanctuary of S. Venera, where Aphrodite (and then, in Roman times, Venus) was adored, has been carefully investigated by a recent Italian-American expedition. It lies on the south-east side of the city, immediately outside the walls, on the banks of a creek flowing down from the Capaccio mountains, called Salso or Capodifiume.

Most of the building remains go back to Roman-age rebuilding in the area, but recent studies have shed light on the more ancient phases as well. It is in this sanctuary that the well-known metope of Heracles on the bull, datable around 520 B.C. and presently in the Naples Museum, was found.

The most important monumental phase dates to the fifth century, when the cult building was erected. Its plan has the form of a rectangle in which a circle is inscribed. The necropolises of Greek Poseidonia mostly lie to the north (at the east and west extremities of the city) and to the south. To the north-east lies the necropolis of Laghetto, which has yielded the most ancient grave-goods, attributable to the first generation of colonists from Sybaris. The graves of the other northern necropolis, lying to the north-west of the city, in Arcioni, are generally very simple, consisting of a pit dug into the earth and covered with a double-pitch roofing made of tiles. The grave-goods include vases from Corinthian workshops.

A few hundred meters south of the sanctuary of S. Venera is the great southern necropolis, prevalently used during the 5th century B.C. The burials, consisting of pits dug into the rock bank and covered with a rock slab, are laid out with striking precision along regular axes and delimited by narrow streets allowing passage through the graveyard. The grave-goods, in conformity with the typical customs of this period, are extremely sober.

Poseidonia.
Tomb 175 of the
necropolis of S. Venera.
Attic red-figured pelike
with a Satyr and
Dionysus.
470 B.C. ca.

13

2. COMMUNITIES AND CULTURES OF SOUTHERN CAMPANIA

The southern part of ancient Campania was involved, at the time of the foundation of Poseidonia, in a process of social change whose main protagonists were the Etruscans. From the beginning of the 6th century B.C., alongside with the more ancient and southernmost settlement corresponding to present-day Pontecagnano, new Etruscan cities were founded in the Sorrentine peninsula and in the northernmost part of the Poseidoniate gulf, the present-day Gulf of Salerno, both on the coast (Castellammare, Vico Equense, Vietri sul Mare) and inland, in nodal points along important communication routes (Pompeii, Nola, Nocera, Fratte).

A culturally homogeneous environment thus extended down to the right bank of the Sele and confronted the imposing presence of the Greek city of Poseidonia. The function of the *Heraion* at the mouth of the Sele, the most ancient and important of the sanctuaries placed at the margins of the territory of Poseidonia, thus becomes clearer. It was a sort of spiritual stronghold against the non-Greek communities residing on the opposite bank of the river, the material expression of a limit, a frontier between Greek and Etruscan supremacy.

This limit, however, did not entail a sharp separation between two mutually incompatible worlds. On the contrary, it was a concrete sign of the complexity of a reality in which the cohabitation of different economic and social entities generated phenomena of osmosis and trends towards cultural uniformity.

The archaeological evidence of Poseidonia thus poses

14

several problems of interpretation, due to the complexity
of the processes set in motion by the foundation of the
colonies. One cannot downplay the influence on the city
of the nearby Etruscan or Etruscanized communities.

The elements of knowledge in our possession show that,
towards the end of the 6th century B.C., the Greek city
was extremely vital and a center of attraction for all the
non-Greek communities residing on the gulf of
Poseidonia. After Croton destroyed its mother-town
Sybaris, Poseidonia apparently sought to control the indigenous world from the inside, and strengthened its role as
an intermediary between the Achaean cities of the Ionian
coast, especially Metapontum, the Enotrian communities,
the Campanian centers of the Salerno plain and Capua.

At the same time, the Etruscanized areas of southern
Campania show intense social mobility, weaving relations
with Greeks, Etruscans and Italics that often gave rise to
mixed communities, i.e. to structured realities in which
ethnically different groups and individuals not only coha-
bited, but also apparently coalesced politically, although
the Etruscan element generally seems to have prevailed.

The best known example of such a community is Fratte, a
settlement lying on the river Irno, at a nodal point along
an inland itinerary leading to Poseidonia to the south and
connecting the plain of Salerno with the Sarno river valley
and the Capuan plain.

From the last quarter of the 6th and for all the first half of
the following century, Fratte went through a remarkable
process of development, reflected both by the necropolis,
with its rich eminent burials, with grave-goods comprising
high-quality Attic black- and red-figured vases, Etruscan
pottery and bronze utensils, and by the monumentalizing
of the town.

The hill of Scigliato became the acropolis of the settlement, featuring paved streets running along large and
imposing buildings whose roofs were decorated by poly-
chrome terracottas of a type diffused over all the Campanian territory.

To one of these buildings with stone walls, possibly an
Etruscan-type temple, belong some architectural frag-

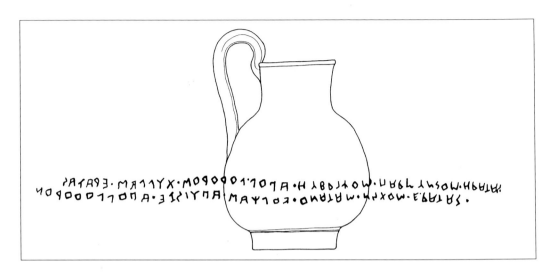

*Fratte.
Small black-painted
olpe with a two-line
retrograde Greek
inscription in Achaean
dialect, reading:
"Apollodorus loves
Ksylla, Vulca commits
sodomy on Apollodorus,
Onas loves Niksos,
Ybricos has loved
Parmynius".
480-460 B.C.*

ments whose fabrication, for reasons of style, must be attributed to Poseidoniate craftsmen, just as a terracotta male statue found near Fratte is stylistically so similar to a Poseidoniate one representing an enthroned male deity, Zeus or Poseidon, that it can be supposed they were made in the same workshop.

Along with its monuments and objects, the inscriptions of Fratte, comprising not only Greek and Etruscan inscriptions, but also the names of Italics written in Oscan, in Greek or in Etruscan, are the most eloquent testimony of the different cultural and ethnic components that settled and organized themselves politically in this center in the 5th century B.C.

A very important example is one impressed in the raw clay of a small black-painted olpe from a Fratte tomb, made in Poseidonia at the beginning of the 5th century. It celebrates in verses erotic games between Greek, Etruscan and Italic characters whose names are Apollodorus, Onata, Vulca, Hybricus and Parmyinius. This inscription evokes the sphere of the symposium where, through the ritual governing the consumption of wine, the drink sacred to the god Dionysus, the participants established personal relationships often having other, more complex implications as well.

These extraordinary phenomena of integration are attested in Poseidonia itself through other documents as well, e.g. the Etruscan-type roofs dated between the end of the 6th and the beginning of the 5th century B.C., possibly a vestige of Etruscan-type sacred buildings in the area of the southern sanctuary of the Greek city.

The "Tomb of the Diver" is the most explicit document of the osmosis between colonial Greeks and the elites of the numerous and variegated neighbouring communities.

This tomb, datable around 470/480 B.C., is the only one found in a Greek city to have the internal walls of the chest and the lid decorated with figured scenes, a custom that, on the other hand, is attested in Etruria as early as the Archaic age.

The pictorial decorative program of this extraordinary document, with its play of reciprocal allusions between the symposium scene represented on the side walls and the image of the diver on the lid gives the impression of a wish to fuse visually and conceptually the values that made a Greek citizen noble and a metaphorical representation of the passage into the Beyond.

The identification of the individual buried here still remains an unsolved problem. The tomb itself is anomalous with respect to Greek culture, which ignores the custom of decorating with paintings the internal walls of burials and, above all, keeps strictly apart, almost as if they were in opposition, the world of death from that of

Poseidonia. Tomb of the Diver in the necropolis of Tempa del Prete. North slab. Cover slab with the scene of the dive.
480 B.C. ca.

17

the symposium. It is possible that the "Tomb of the Diver" (which, unsurprisingly, does not belong to the necropolis, having been found in a farm south of the city, in a locality called Tempa del Prete) belonged to an individual of a family group that was not integrated among the citizens of Poseidonia. It represents a deviation from the norm that is also a sign of political integration. The buried individual chose to give an individual answer to death by exalting, through the scenes of the symposium, other forms of integration. The codes and models used correspond perfectly to those governing the symposium in the Greek city but, in this exceptional case, the pleasure of wine-drinking is unequivocally projected beyond life.

Although not so overtly as the Tomb of the diver, about twenty burials of the urban necropolis of Poseidonia also deviate from the norm. Their grave-goods, besides the usual objects, prevalently vases used to contain perfumed oils, include some vase forms not belonging to the Greek repertory, such as small impasto jars decorated by a row of bosses under the rim and a fine-ware mug with a surmounting handle, s very common object in Etruscan-Campanian sites, more specifically in Nola, Vico Equense, Nocera and Fratte.

Another anomaly is represented by tombs belonging to inhumed women laid in a supine-contracted position typical of the indigenous communities residing at the edges of the Vallo di Diano.

These apparently insignificant data, when abstracted from the entire context of Poseidonia and its neighbouring territories, are the most eloquent testimony of complex social dynamics that, if they are well interpreted and understood, free Antiquity of the exotic character a by now stale culture has insisted in attributing to it and help us to reconstruct human vicissitudes in which our own history is rooted.

19

*Poseidonia. Tomb
of the Diver in the
necropolis of Tempa
del Prete. North slab.
Detail of the
convivial scene.
480 B.C. ca.*

3. SAMNITES AND LUCANIANS FROM THE GULF OF POSEIDONIA TO THE GULF OF LAOS (SCALEA, CALABRIA)

According to the ancient historian Strabo, Lucania extended from the Tyrrhenian coast between the Sele and the Laos to the Ionian coast between Metapontum and Thurii. This has been confirmed by the studies and field-work of the last twenty years, which have brought a decisive contribution to our knowledge of this ancient region.

The emerging of the Lucanian *ethnos* on the political scene is the result of a long process beginning when Croton destroyed Sybaris at the end of the 6th century B.C. The downfall of Sybaris' empire had fired off struggles for the control of its territory, provoking tensions between the Greek cities, internally rent by political discord. This situation eventually favored the indigenous communities, whose political breakthrough was determined by the insertion in their midst of warriors, possibly mercenaries. At the end of this period, the literary sources mention the attacks of the Lucanians against the newly-founded city of Thurii and Poseidonia's alliance, in its struggle against Velia, with groups of Italics.

The Lucanians' appearance on the 5th-century political scene thus cannot depend exclusively on the descent of groups of people from the Samnium. It is rather the result of a dynamic process in which the indigenous communities were transformed by protracted contacts with the Greek colonies, with the Oscan people of Etruscanized Campania and with the Apulians.

The individual centers reacted to this process in different ways, as the culture of some changed dramatically, while in others the transformation took the form of a gradual evolution. From this period on, and for all of the following century, many settlements lying on the Tyrrhenian, especially Eboli and Pontecagnano, came to new life. Inland sites such as Buccino and Satriano went through a process of transformation, assuming a more elaborate territorial organization, a reflection of an increasingly complex social stratification.

*Buccino. Tomb 270
in Santo Stefano.
Silver kantharos.
End of the
4th century B.C.*

PONTECAGNANO

The story of the settlement of the area of the present-day town of Pontecagnano, a few kilometers north of the Sele, begins in the 9th century B.C., when its territory was occupied by a community belonging to the culture called "Villanovian" (the protohistoric predecessors of the Etruscans). In the course of the 8th and the beginning of the 7th century B.C., this center enjoyed a period of special prosperity due to its role as an emporium, i.e. a commercial port of call, open to trade with all the Mediterranean. At the end of the 7th century, the founda-

21

tion of Poseidonia somewhat undermined Pontecagnano's commercial role, although it did not bring about its decline. The crisis that hit coastal Etruria from the second quarter of the 5th century, also affecting the center of Pontecagnano, occurred at the same time as a wider political process involving the entire region of Campania and leading to the formation of new political entities, viz. the Samnites, the Campanians and the Lucanians.

As in the preceding phases of Pontecagnano's history, the most valid instrument for the evaluation of the Samnite period is the analysis of the necropolis, whose systematic exploration has provided an exceptionally representative sample.

The tombs of the end of the 5th and the first half of the 4th century B.C., which continue to occupy the planned burial grounds of the 8th century, reveal the existence of a well-defined social structure. The "gentile" cemetery in via Sicilia, including tombs dating from the 8th to the beginning of the 5th century B.C., is an exceptionally well-preserved testimony of the continuity and the development of the buried group. From the second quarter of the 5th century B.C., the funerary area was extended towards the west into an area which had previously been used only sporadically. This area was used intensively during the 4th century, while later on the number of burials tends to decrease. Other sepulchral areas begin to be exploited intensively from the second quarter of the 4th century (a time when the Via Sicilia nucleus seems to decline) and present an unbroken continuity until the eve of the foundation of Picentia (268 B.C.). They may belong to new groups, distinct with respect to the urban community. Their appearance seems to coincide with a crisis in the settlement system of the ancient city. Tomb 6214 is especially remarkable. It is a travertine chest burial belonging to a male whose only grave-goods were two belts. Like Poseidoniate tombs, its interior is decorated with paintings representing griffins and panthers.

Recent excavations in the settlement area have revealed that, at Pontecagnano, as in other centers of southern Campania, urban restructuring was in course.

EBOLI

Throughout ancient history, Eboli was a crossroads whose importance varied from one historical period to the other, being located at the border between two different cultural areas, and at the confluence of two natural routes, the Tusciano river valley and the more important Ofanto-Sele road. In the 9th and 8th centuries B.C., the culture of Eboli was mainly Villanovian.

The archaeological evidence, however, also indicates the presence, from the middle of the 8th century or earlier, of groups whose culture is different both in its funerary ritual and in its material manifestations, which are typical of the so-called "fossa-tomb culture" of Tyrrhenian southern Italy. The cohabitation of groups belonging to different cultures, due to the special position of the settlement, also continued in the following period. This is documented by burials of individuals from the nearby middle valley of the Sele.

The foundation of Poseidonia deprived Pontecagnano of control of the Ofanto itinerary, which was now controlled by the Etruscan settlement of Fratte. This new state of things also affected Eboli, whose necropolises appear essentially uniform in this period, although, from the middle of the 6th century B.C., isolated eminent burials occur, with grave-goods including abundant Corinthian and Attic pottery and inscriptions.

In the course of the 5th century B.C., the size of the necropolis decreased markedly. In the few tombs dating from this period, the composition of burial equipment reflects traditions attested in the towns of the middle course of the Sele. The inscriptions attest the survival of Etruscan, and are written in the Achaean alphabet used in Poseidonia, confirming the existence of relations between the Greek city and the indigenous populations of the adjoining territories. Unlike some of its neighbours, among whom these contacts stimulated the coming to the fore of eminent individuals, Eboli remained a marginal reality, leaning towards the conservative cultures of its inland neighbors.

Shortly before the middle of the 4th century, Eboli went through remarkable changes, mainly documented by its necropolises, which extended to occupy new areas at the foot of the Montedoro. The burials, grouped in clusters separated

23

by ample empty spaces, are not laid out according to a well-defined plan, but are gathered around one or more eminent burials. The latter are distinguished by the quality and typology of their grave-goods, apparently reflecting a division of society into kinship groups comprising adult males strongly connoted as warriors by the presence in their graves of a spear and a belt, gathering around chiefs whose burials feature bronze panoplies (complete armour) and throwing weapons. Some individuals are identified as riders by miniature bronze spurs and iron horse-bits. An exceptional example of a burial of such a "military chief" is provided by tomb 37, found in Santa Croce.

Its vase-kit is prevalently composed of the wine-drinking set, comprising a red-figured crater of Paestan production, a freight amphora, vases used for drinking and as ladles, and bronze vases (basin, situla, cup, mug, *oinochoe*). It also contained objects evoking the domestic sphere, viz. fireplace instruments (andirons and spits), mostly made of lead, and terracotta objects reproducing the fruits of the earth and cakes, a symbol of agrarian wealth. The "wealthiest" female burials, lying near those of males with complete armor, are distinguished especially by the presence of ornaments (rings and bronze or silver fibulae). Their vase-kits generally include a Paestan-made red-figured *hydria* (a vase used as a water container) and a set including a *skyphos* and an *oinochoe*, i.e. the drinking and pouring vases with which the women represented on the Paestum painted slabs greet the victorious warrior. Nuptial

Eboli. Tomb 37 in Santa Croce. Bronze vases. Middle of the 4th century B.C. ca.

lebes, made of separate assembled parts, are found only in a few eminent burials also containing the lead fireplace instruments and the terracottas reproducing fruit and rural products. In the late 4th century B.C., a fortified enclosure was erected on the peak of Montedoro.

There was no settlement inside it, but it was used by the groups who buried their dead at its foot, possibly to be identified with all or part of the *Eburini*, whom Pliny includes among the Lucanians.

BUCCINO

After being the site of a Neolithic settlement, this area was occupied by an important Early Bronze Age village discovered in the locality presently called Tufariello. Between the end of the 7th and the first decades of the 4th century B.C., in the area presently occupied by the historical centre of the present-day town, several necropolises document a regional *facies* called "Platano valley culture", characterized by a formal and decorative repertory similar to that of the sites of Atena Lucana, Satriano and Ruvo del Monte, and by the custom of burying the dead in a contracted position. The

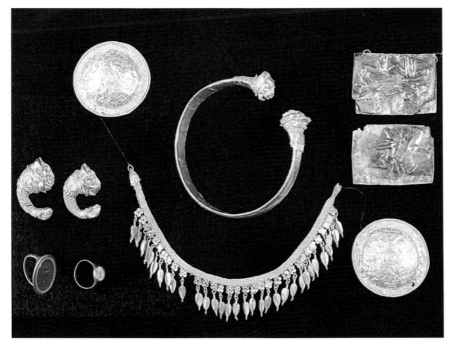

Buccino. Tomb 270 in Santo Stefano. Golden female ornaments. End of the 4th century B.C.

25

Buccino. Tomb 270 in Santo Stefano. Detail of the bronze basin. 4th century B.C.

most conspicuous sign of a strong cultural change is the passage from this funerary ritual to one in which the body is deposed in a supine position. This evolution is more or less contemporary with the construction of city walls in limestone *opus quadratum* datable to the 4th century B.C. An area in a locality called Santo Stefano, where archaeological investigations have revealed a remarkable continuity of use, is especially interesting. Here, in the course of the 4th century B.C., buildings with a rather elaborate plan were erected between and next to necropolis areas. In the latter,

Buccino. Tomb 270 in Santo Stefano. Carnelian stone representing Aphrodite and an eros. End of the 4th century B.C.

a painted chamber tomb stands out. Its paintings represent a chariot race, and its grave-goods include fragments of a vase signed by Assteas, the second Paestan ceramographer known to us. One of the most remarkable burials of this period is tomb 270, made of limestone blocks, datable to the end of the 4th century B.C., and attributable to a woman. Her burial equipment was quite rich, featuring jewellery, probably of Tarentine production, and precious metal vases.

ROSCIGNO

About two kilometers north-east of the modern town lies Mount Pruno (879 meters above sea-level), the extreme south-west outpost of the Alburni mountain chain, dominating the only pass connecting the Vallo di Diano with the fertile Paestan plain. On its plateau, some burials dating from the 6th century B.C. indicate the presence of a community dispersed in scattered nuclei.

Another interesting burial, datable to the 5th century, was recently found. It contained rich metallic grave-goods, including a situla, a basin, a bronze *oinochoe* and a group of iron spits, plus several weapons, viz. two bronze helmets, a sword and two spearheads.

A tomb found on the plateau in 1938 (called "princely" because of the wealth displayed by its burial equipment), unlike previous tombs, in which the corpse lay in a contracted position, contained a supine body.

Along its right side were a candelabrum, a bronze *nestoris*, a silver *kantharos*, a crater decorated with a columned motif and bronze strigils; at its foot, numerous black-painted vases, the remains of a chariot, a *rhyton* and a red-figured *kylix*, both Attic, and two red-figured *oinochoai* of proto-Italiot production; on its left side, bronze vases, including a *Schnabelkanne* with an oblique beak, an olpe with a Gorgon-head at the lower extremity of the handle, a small olpe, a mug, a sieve, five basins, a grater and a lamp. This rich burial equipment also includes a silver crown.

The silver *kantharos* is especially remarkable. It is decorated with two gilded-silver Silenic heads and inside, on the bottom, with an embossed motif, also of gilded silver, with a studded contour like that of a coin, representing an

27

*Roscigno.
"Princely" tomb
of Monte Pruno. Silver
kantharos. End of the
5th century B.C.*

Amazon with fluttering chiton and cloak. In exergue, the name ANDPOMAXA *Andromaca* is inscribed in Doric dialect. Several of the objects are Etruscan-made, viz. the candelabrum (whose stem is decorated, at its upper extremity, with a warrior with his left arm around the shoulders of the woman beside him), the olpe with the Gorgon-head at the lower extremity of the handle, the other small olpe decorated with floral motifs and the sieve. The mug and the great basin are of Great Greek production. The bronze *nestoris*, with its incised floral decoration, is an *unicum*. It is a typical vase of indigenous tradition, similar to a crater and characterized by vertical handles decorated by discs rising far above the rim. This burial equipment, as a whole, indicates that the deceased adhered to Greek models. This is especially borne out by the absence of weapons, with the exception of a spearhead, and by the evocation of the banquet and of athletic practices.

Not far from here, in a locality called Cuozzi, in the second half of the 4th century B.C., an elaborate building compound was constructed, which remained in use at least until the last decades of the 3rd century B.C. It consisted of rooms arranged around a vast central court and extended over an area between 400 and 500 square meters, being hence comparable, both in plan and in dimensions, with the Roccagloriosa compounds. Archaeologists also brought to light a small furnace adjoining the building, used for the production of cooking vessels, unpainted containers, black-painted pottery, loom-weights and *louteria*. Further uphill, several half-chamber burials were discovered. The best preserved one is tomb 3200, with a rectangular enclosure and a floor covered by a thin layer of clay. The corpse lay in a contracted position on its right side, and almost all the grave-goods were on the southern side of the enclosure. The bronze vases (a situla and a small olpe were recovered), the non-functional metallic instruments (lead andirons and spits) and especially the vase-kit, comprising quite a few Paestan-made specimens, reflect an ideological system well attested and diffused in the neighboring territories. On the other hand, the persistence of the use of a contracted position for the body (indicated by the arms being crossed and by the position of the body on its left side) is rather anomalous, as, in the other necropolises of the same area, inhumation in a supine position had by this time become the norm.

The town walls of the settlement have been recently explored. They are made of rectangular blocks of local limestone and rest on foundations obtained by cutting and adapting the rocky slopes at different altitudes to exploit natural contour lines.

Their construction goes back to the second half of the 4th century B.C., a period when the settlement pattern changed, although an organization in scattered nuclei still prevailed. In this period, funerary ritual appears essentially continuous, although both the composition of burial equipment and the individual grave-goods indicate that relations with the Paestan area had become more intense.

As many other Lucanian-age settlements of inland Campania and Lucania, Roscigno also shows clear signs of

Roscigno. "Princely" tomb of Monte Pruno. Detail of the cyma of the bronze candelabrum. End of the 5th century B.C.

29

Roscigno. "Princely" tomb of Monte Pruno. Detail of the bronze olpe. End of the 5th century B.C.

*Roscigno.
"Princely" tomb
of Monte Pruno.
Nestoris. End of the
5th century B.C.*

having been suddenly abandoned at the end of the 3rd century B.C., when Roman presence was beginning to manifest itself in this area.

SATRIANO

The hill of Satriano (about
950 meters above sea-level
and 20 kilometers south-west
of Potenza) dominates a very
important network of natural
routes, as it overlooks the itinerary leading to the Vallo di
Diano and Campania on one
side and the one leading to
the Ionian coast on the other.
From the 6th century B.C., a
settlement area is attested at
the foot of the hill, fortified,
at the end of the century, by a
fence that was further extended towards the end of the
5th and beginning of the 4th
century B.C. At the end of the
4th century B.C., the settlement was abandoned, and an
enclosure wall of squared stone blocks was built on the
acropolis, transforming the top of the hill in a fortress
enclosing no other buildings.

The necropolises, dating from the end of the 7th to the
beginning of the 4th century B.C., lie in a ring around the
hill. In one of the most recent investigations on the north-
western slopes of the hill, six tombs, datable between the
end of the 6th and the last quarter of the 5th, were brought to light.

One of them, belonging to a warrior, contained an
Apulian-Corinthian bronze helmet, an iron sword and a
vase-kit datable to the first quarter of the 5th century
B.C. North-west of the hill, near a spring, a sanctuary was

discovered: its rectangular hall (13 x 3 meters) had a porticoed facade and was divided into two rooms of different sizes by a dividing wall. The smaller room lying east, due to the presence of burnt remains and of fragments of terracotta braziers, has been identified as a kitchen, the larger one lying east as a banquet room. On the exterior, near the entrance of this "banquet room", a small sandstone pillar and a bronze *phiale mesomphalos* were found. Many clues suggest these two objects were associated, as the pillar may have served as a support for the *phiale* used by the lady of the house to perform libations. Adjoining one of the long sides of this building is a square *sacellum* (4,70 by 4,40 meters) in which numerous votive offerings were deposed, including coins from Great Greek and Roman mints, the latter dated after 211 B.C.

The whole area was surrounded by an enclosure whose traces have been found both east and south of the sanctuary. At the end of the 3rd century B.C., the spot was abandoned and no longer frequented until the 1st century B.C., when the area was reoccupied and rebuilt.

The drainage system, two fountains and an altar seem to belong to this phase. A dry-stone enclosure, possibly a corral, dates from the 4th century A.D. In late Roman or medieval times, the area was occupied by a necropolis.

Satriano. Sanctuary in Torre. The small pillar and the phiale. 4th century B.C.

31

ROCCAGLORIOSA

The site of Roccagloriosa, lying on the slopes of Mount Capitenali, dominates the entire Gulf of Policastro. The site was frequented as early as the Neolithic period, during the Bronze Age and in the Archaic period. Traces of constructions interpreted as hut floors are datable between the 7th and the 6th century B.C. On the central plateau, in the course of the 5th century B.C., the first permanent settlements appears. The houses have a rectangular elongated plan, stone foundations and internal partitions whose original structural complexity is suggested by the fictile architectural decoration recovered. It is the burials, however, that provide the clearest picture of the transformations taking place between the end of the 5th and during the 4th century B.C., with the emerging of aristocratic groups.

In the course of the 4th century B.C., on the terraces shelving down towards the sea, a number of settlement nuclei were discovered, documenting a dense occupation of the countryside. Around the middle of the 4th century, on the crest of Mount Capitenali, a fortification enclosing no less than 15 hectares was built. Inside it were three settlement nuclei, at a considerable distance one from the other. Another building built on the central plateau, going back to the first quarter of the 4th century, consists of a rectangular structure with a series of rooms arranged around a central court enclosed by a columned portico. In the north-east corner of this court was a *naiskos* (edicule) with its altar facing the main entrance. Inside it, numerous sta-

Roccagloriosa. Tomb 9 in La Scala. Gold and silver ornaments. 360 B.C. ca.

32

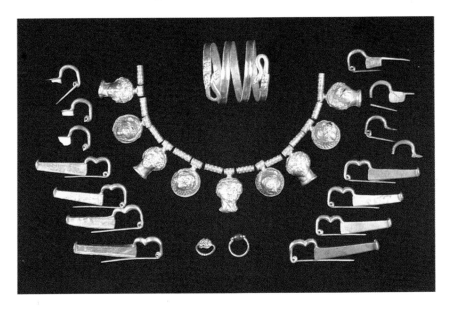

tuettes were found, including a Poseidoniate-made one representing Hera wearing the *polos* and the *phiale*, and the remains of goat and sheep sacrifices. This *naiskos* continued to be used until the last quarter of the century.

The necropolis of "La Scala", lying right outside the fortified settlement area, was clearly intended for the burial of the members of the aristocratic groups living inside the walls. Male tombs 6 and 10, each placed at the center of a cluster of tombs, belonged to clan elders. Their grave-goods include a precious bronze set of vases, mostly of Etruscan provenance, similar to those found in inland Lucania and especially in the Roscigno tombs. A few chamber tombs date from the second half of the 4th century B.C., while at the end of the same century some individuals had themselves cremated (*ustrina* tombs). Tomb 9, whose most striking feature is its ostentation of gold objects and personal ornaments, is contemporary with the monumentalizing of the compound.

LAOS

The ancient historian Strabo concludes his description of Tyrrhenian Lucania with the city of Laos which, together with Skidros, was the residence of the Sybarite exiles after the destruction of Sybaris in 510 B.C. Almost nothing is known of the Greek city, with the exception of a series of incused silver coins of the first half of the century, made with Sybarite types and inscribed with Achaean letters. The written sources also tell us that, in 39 B.C., Laos was a flourishing Lucanian center, and it is likely that the city they mention is the same as the Greek one. In the last third of the 4th century B.C., the city was founded anew on the hill of San Bartolo, south of the mouth of the river Laos, on a vast hill plateau enclosed by imposing fortifications. The settlement was organized according to a Greek-type urban layout, with two north-south streets of considerable width (*plateiai*) crossing six orthogonal streets. The explored houses overlook the largest of the *plateiai*. They are built around large open courts, often elaborately decorated, in some of which the remains of productive activities were found. In one building in particular, among

33

34

Laos (Marcellina).
Chamber tomb.
Anatomical cuirass.
330-320 B.C.

a great quantity of cinders and small unidentified fragments of lead, bronze and iron, 23 uncoined bronze discs were found, of the same weight and size as the bronze coins of the 3rd century Laotian series. These data suggest the building was a mint, and must have hence lain near the agora, which has not been identified as yet.

The necropolises of Laos are not well known. One group, composed of poor fossa tombs, lay near the Marcellina railroad station. In the same area, in 1962, a chamber tomb containing two bodies was discovered. Its grave-goods are the result of protracted accumulation, as the most ancient pieces go back to 380-370, while the burial is of 330-320 B.C. The two buried individuals, a men and a woman, lay in wooden sarcophagi accompanied by their status-symbols. The tomb contained the remains of a horse (with no harness or tacks), a sign that the deceased belonged to the equestrian order. Among the man's grave-goods was a complete armour composed of a Phrygian-type helmet, a belt, greaves and an anatomical cuirass with a Medusa-protome mask embossed on the front and a satyr protome on the back.

One of the most remarkable of these grave-goods is a lead tablet with an inscription containing invectives (*defixio*) against the city magistrates. It is likely that these invectives reflect the social tension that must have existed at the time between the aristocratic groups the two tomb-owners belonged to and the new "democratic" institutions of the Lucanians. In the 3rd century B.C., as a consequence of the war against Hannibal, the city was abandoned and no longer reoccupied.

35

4. THE LUCANIANS IN PAESTUM

LUCANIAN MERCENARIES IN GREEK POSEIDONIA

In the necropolises of Poseidonia, at the end of the 5th century B.C., the burial ritual shows signs of radical change, due to the adoption of practices which are completely foreign to Greek mentality and customs.

The sobriety of traditional burials gives way to a tendency towards the accumulation and ostentation of wealth, and a wish to stress the "status" and rank of buried individuals through grave-goods.

This sharp discontinuity has been interpreted as one of the signs of the conquest of Poseidonia by the Lucanians,

Paestum. Gaudo necropolis, tomb 259. Burial equipment. 410-440.

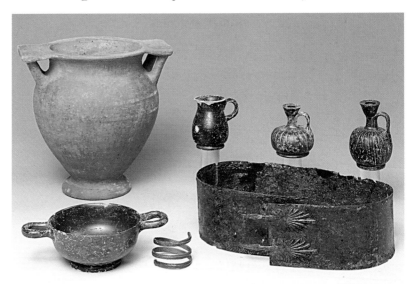

mentioned by the Greek geographer Strabo in a famous passage (V, 4, 13). The most recent results of archaeological research have confirmed the validity of this interpretation, providing further information on the crucial period, spanning of a few decades, immediately preceding the Lucanians' rise to power. In these years, organized groups of outsiders, which seemed to coalesce, as in the Samnite custom, around armed individuals, settled in the northern suburb of Poseidonia.

The only evidence we have of these people is their necropolis, which lies along the axis connecting Poseidonia to the sanctuary of Hera at the mouth of the Sele, about 500 meters north-west of the city, in the locality called Gaudo. Shortly after the middle of the 5th century B.C., the newcomers began to bury their dead here, although without encroaching on the pre-existing cemeteries (500-470/60 B.C.) of small, no longer active extra-urban settlements.

The graves are arranged in roughly circular or semicircular groups, whose center is occupied by a burial distinguished either by specific architectural characteristics or by its grave-goods.

The most ancient depositions (440/420 B.C.) are characterized by a burial ritual and a material culture presenting many similarities with the late 5th century B.C. necropolises of Samnitized Campania. In particular, rather close parallels can be drawn, in the ideology revealed by the composition of burial equipment and funerary ritual, with the Samnite necropolis of Cumae. Here, too, it was customary to lay at the foot of both men and women a jar containing a drinking vase, which in turn held a small jug in its mouth, and, near the body, a plate with painted brown bands on which the remains of animals, mainly sheep, have been found.

These similarities obviously do not allow speculation of any kind. One can only acknowledge the existence, within two distinct Greek-type urban realities of the Tyrrhenian *paralía* (coast), of unrelated groups with a culturally similar behavior.

It is more difficult to assess the nature and importance, within the group, of inland indigenous elements. Only a

37

Paestum. Gaudo necropolis, tomb 268. Amber necklace with a glaze pendant. 420-400 B.C.

few individuals, mostly, but not exclusively female, present a dress or objects typical of Western Lucania, such as the *nestoris* or the *trozzella*. A high number of male tombs, identified by the javelin, tend to cluster around lance or javelin-bearers wearing the "Samnite" sword-belt or the three-disc bivalve cuirass. It is not improbable that these individuals were professional warriors, mercenaries hired by the polis and residing in the city in a marginal position, who apparently gathered around themselves a following of locals from the neighbouring territories. Similar behavior patterns are attested in nearby Campania as well.

Among the burial clusters thus connoted, a single tomb stands out. It lies, physically speaking, at the edges of the burial ground, and belongs to a male, between 50 and 60 years old, devoid of grave-goods, with the exception of four functional iron fibulae to close the garment which he wore when he was buried. The presence of these fibulae, i.e. of objects generally found only in

Paestum. Gaudo necropolis, tomb 136. Belt decorated with a lamina on which a panther attacking a deer is represented. 420-480 B.C.

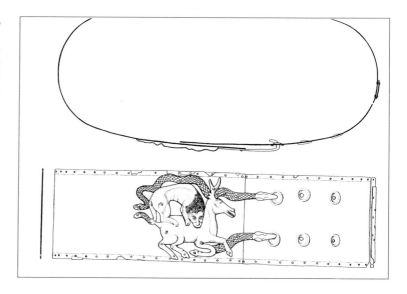

female depositions, this necropolis being no exception, is only one of the peculiar features of this burial. The special status of the buried individual is further emphasized by the decoration of the inside of the lid covering the tomb where, for the exclusive benefit of the deceased, right in front of his face (which was held up by a sort of rock cushion), a *prosopon* was sculpted, i.e. a face, in very low relief, with animal ears and a short pointed beard, which can be regarded as a representation, in a language very far removed from Greek tradition, of a Silenus. It is not possible to deal here with

Paestum. Gaudo necropolis, tomb 315, the so-called "tomb of the shaman". Detail of the covering slab. End of the 5th century B.C.

the possible implications of the Silenic image in this particular context. It is however worth stressing the significance of the presence, in a marginal position with respect to the group, of a man bearing signs (the fibulae) typical of the female sphere, thus seeming to embody, as is typical of shamanic figures, the opposition between the sexes, and accompanied by a figure belonging, if it has been correctly interpreted, to the Dionysiac imagery, placed face to face with him, in a confrontation beginning immediately after the transitory moment of burial.

Poseidonia, in the second half of the 5th century – at the time of its war with Velia, if Strabo's indication (VI,1,1) actually refers to this period – granted to these people, whose most distinctive characteristic is their hierarchical military organization, the permission to settle in its suburbs and to bury their dead on its land. We know nothing of their social organization. The arrangement of their graves in clusters around a burial taking on a central role seems a projection of some sort of family organization. On the other hand, the layout of certain sectors of the necropolis, occupied almost exclusively by armed men displaying a hierarchy of functions, seems to reflect other patterns of organization as well.

Whatever the role of these groups in the events that brought about, at the end of the 5th century, the taking over of Poseidonia by the Lucanians (Strabo VI,1,3), the utilization of the necropolis remained continuous, and even increased noticeably between the end of the 5th century B.C. to the first three decades of the following century, although it maintained its marginal, extra-urban character.

The continuity through time of some of these family burial nuclei is one of the most interesting aspects of the necropolis.

The leading figures of these groups, which we can define as true *oikoi* (households), buried in painted tombs or wearing armour, lie side by side with their ancestors, buried with traditional grave-goods, thus projecting their roots backward into the second half of the 5th century and emphasizing parental and hereditary ties. Funerary ritual and grave-goods reflect the changes in the city, defining the role and nature of the buried individuals with increasing precision.

The insistent exalting of the warrior function of the chiefs of the *oikoi*, through the ostentation of armour, and the presence of forms of accumulation and exhibition of wealth-both phenomena that went on, in other sectors of this cemetery, until the late 4th century-set this necropolis sharply apart from the coeval Paestan cemeteries.

The ideological values it seems to reflect were no longer current among the urban community of the first half of the 4th century, but were beginning to be displayed by eminent burials of the necropolises of rural settlements or of neighboring, more closed-up and backward urban communities.

THE PAINTED TOMBS

The Paestan urban necropolises extend outside the northern and southern limits of the city walls, and are called with the modern place-names: Andriuolo, Laghetto and Arcioni to the north, S. Venera, Spinazzo and Licinella to the south.

Around the last decade of the 5th century B.C., the funerary ritual of these necropolises changes completely. The custom of inhuming the dead without grave-goods or with just a few objects gives way to the practice of stressing gender and hierarchical distinctions through the composition of burial equipment.

This change is possibly the most eloquent archaeological testimony of the Lucanians' political occupation of the Greek city. In the male burials, first weapons and then craters (vases used for wine mixing) appear, while the most important female tombs contain jewels and vases such as the hydria (the water container) and the nuptial lebes.

In the tombs of some of these eminent persons, along with these strongly distinctive grave-goods, painted decoration is also present, a feature that is clearly the privilege and the most conspicuous ideological manifestation of the elite. In fact, out of a thousand burials spanning the entire 4th century B.C., only eighty are painted, and about fifty of these lay in the urban necropolises, mainly in that of Andriuolo.

The grave-goods and the pictorial decoration of the Paestan necropolis are an exceptional document of the history of the city in the period of Lucanian domination, on which no written sources exist.

The paintings themselves are not mere decorative elements, as they reflect the values and ideals of the hegemonic groups of Paestum between the end of the 5th and the first decades of the 3rd century B.C. As part of a funerary ritual reserved to high-ranking persons, the paintings were quickly executed on the spot, using a technique very similar to that of frescoes, and were meant to be seen by the living only during the funeral.

41

Hence, although they often do not attain a high artistic level, they are an extraordinary ethnographic document. Through these images we become acquainted with the central values of this society which, in forms typical of archaic mentalities, puts itself on the stage at the crucial moment of death, projecting an ideal image of itself.

That the purpose of tomb decoration was not purely decorative is further confirmed by the fact that, although they display variations in style and taste, the scenes repeat themselves from tomb to tomb, and the elements occupying the four walls of each chamber are not arran-

Paestum. Gaudo necropolis, tomb 265. West slab. 370-350 B.C.

42

ged in a casual order, but according to fixed patterns making up an actual decorative program. Through the internal play of their associations, the images function as a language that takes form and unfolds in the short lapse of time in which the paintings are executed.

The transition from the earlier tombs decorated with painted bands, mostly found in the necropolises of the Paestan territory (Gaudo, Tempa del Prete), to those featuring figured scenes is heralded by the appearance, at the beginning of the 4th century B.C., in the urban necropolis of Andriuolo, of vegetable and animal motifs, or of objects depicted in the white central space of one or more walls of the tomb.

Paestum. Andriuolo necropolis, tomb 21/1969. East slab: tree and birds. 380 B.C.

These objects represent those actually deposed as grave-goods in the burials, and thus allude to the funerary ritual. Tomb 21 features a particular scene representing an animate motif, a laurel tree on whose branches an owl and a black bird are perched and toward which two more birds are flying. The slab on which this scene appears presents, as the other three from the same tomb, geometrically organized spaces, with a high black socle and a frame decorated by two tree branches converging towards a rosette. The animate motif was probably executed with the same technique and probably the same cartoons used by the ceramists.

In the first quarter of the 4th century B.C., it became common to decorate tomb walls with more complex scenes centered on human figures. The emblematic image of military valour, a fundamental value for this Lucanian

43

Paestum. Andriuolo necropolis, tomb 11/1969. East slab: the return of the warrior. 350-340 B.C.

community, was created for male tombs, viz. the "return of the warrior", in which the rider, loaded with weapons seized from the enemy, returns to his community and is greeted by a woman who holds out to him the objects used for libations.

This scene is associated with representations of funerary games occupying the long sides, the chariot race on one slab, the "boxing match" and the "duel" on the other. These scenes evoke the traditional aristocratic rite of funerary games stressing the importance of the deceased. They represent the final moment of the competition, designating the winner and the loser. In the chariot race, the column drawn at the center of the slab represents the post around which the chariots curve. In the boxing scenes, a flute-player plays rhythm to the match, whose violence is indicated by the blood running down the boxers' faces. In the duels, a judge stands beside the winner, about to place a wreath on his head.

Funerary games are also depicted in female tombs, where the image of the return of the warrior is absent, being replaced by a great wreath (duplicated on the facing short slab) or by a deer-hunting scene.

Stylistically speaking, the figures are monumental, and are exalted by the red socle they stand upon. Their contours are highlighted by sharp and repetitive contrasts of

Paestum. Laghetto necropolis, tomb X. North slab: chariot race. 350 B.C. ca.

45

Paestum. Andriuolo necropolis, tomb 12/1969. South slab: boxing and duel.

dull hues of yellow and ochre. Their heads are rather small, with angular profiles, triangular eyes and an almost invisible mouth, while the bodies of the horses are rendered by great spots of color.

Another workshop, contemporary with the more represented and representative one which produced the paintings just described, favors small figures inserted in a space delimited by a well-defined frame, as in a painting. These figures are rendered simply by drawing their contours on the white background of the slab and coloring them with a few touches of red and green. In the composition of the scenes, a taste based on ornamental parameters prevails.

A series of paintings attributable to the other workshop also feature, although their distribution on the slabs is different, duels, boxing matches and wrestling, as well as fliacic characters and female dancers-jugglers that emphasize the games' meaning of "ritual show".

The decorative program of the workshop that conceived the image of the return of the warrior continued to be used, faithfully reproduced or with partial modifications, almost until the end of Paestan pictorial production.

Tomb 1 in Gaudo and chamber-tomb 11 in Contrada Vecchia di Agropoli inaugurate a new style which, although it repeats the older motifs, creates new compositions with grandiose effects obtained through the emphasis of the gestures and the use of very bright colors, well exemplified by the figure of the flute-player in the Gaudo tomb, wearing a long red dress held at the waist by a yellow belt, and with a band, also yellow, holding his cheeks. In the same scene, one of the boxers' face is covered by a half mask with a prominent and beaked nose, tied behind the back of the neck, similar to that of the Neapolitan masked character Pulcinella. These features, also present in other scenes in tombs belonging to necropolises of the northern area of the Paestan territories, emphasize the theatrical aspects of the rites they represent.

Contemporarily with these paintings, from the middle of the 4th century B.C., when Lucanian hegemony was consolidated, new pictorial forms of expressions were also created, based on new figurative repertories and more refined stylistic techniques.

These new approaches were on the one hand grafted onto the old tradition, which conceived the slab as the frame and canvas of a painting, while on the other they generated works of a completely new style, mainly obtained through a play of juxtaposed masses of color.

The most striking innovation is certainly the creation of a figurative program exclusively reserved to female tombs, always belonging to high-ranking women, celebrated through gynaeceum and *prothesis* (exhibition of the corpse) scenes.

The former, through the representation of the female figure, seated in the act of weaving, assisted by a handmaid, establish and exalt the role of the woman as

47

Paestum. Andriuolo necropolis, tomb 47. West slab: exhibition of the corpse. 350 B.C.

mistress of the house and custodian of domestic values. The latter, in depicting the moment of mourning around the deceased stretched out on her funerary bed, wearing sumptuous ornaments, highlight women's function as wives and perpetuators of the family, evoked by children and adolescents appearing alongside the mourning women and the male flute players.

In a totally original and unique way, the succession of paintings of tomb 47 in Andriuolo narrate, as if they were a written text, an actual funerary eulogy in the form of a tale. In the triangle of the fronton of the western slab is the gynaeceum scene, surmounting the *prothesis*, echoed on the opposite slab by a cortege with offering-bearers among whom is a cloaked male figure leading an ox to sacrifice. The narrative sequence is concluded with the scene occupying the small fronton of the eastern slab, where a winged genius with a monstrous face, a combination of the Greek Charon and the Etruscan Vanth, drawn in profile, awaits the deceased woman on a boat to ferry her to the Beyond.

Other tombs feature further variations on the theme of the funerary ritual. Thus, in tomb 53 at Andriuolo, a racing chariot and the duel concluding funerary games are represented on one of the long slabs, the exhibition

Paestum. Andriuolo necropolis, tomb 47. East slab: the voyage of the deceased woman to the Beyond. 350 B.C.

49

of the corpse on the other. On the short slabs, figures are painted only on the small fronton, a rooster on one side and, on the other, a flute-player facing a dwarf buffoon holding a very long spear, recalling the *Miles gloriosus*, the buffoonish soldier of Latin comedy.

The scenes of another group of tombs are centered exclusively on the representation of the funerary ritual. Among these, tomb 8 in Andriuolo stands out. It features the preparation for the funerary exhibition of a child, occupying three slabs, and completed by a scene of eschatological meaning: the god Hermes draws a small carriage on which the child is sitting.

Tomb 61 in Andriuolo is more innovative from a conceptual point of view. Its paintings exalt the role of the inhumed person (a woman, as the grave-goods bear out), through a sequence of images extending over the four slabs, representing the male members of her family in a cortege, ordered by age-group: a youth, a full-grown armed man, a white-haired cloaked man sitting on a carriage drawn by mules. The other slabs feature a duel and a great frieze of weapons next to a rider bearing a trophy consisting of a tunic seized from the enemy, a sign of the importance of the military role of the members of the deceased's family, which was a necessary condition to occupy an eminent position within the community.

This program heralds motifs later to become more explicit in the paintings of the Spinazzo tombs. By defining the harmonious succession of generations and their roles within the hegemonic groups of the Paestan political scene in the second half of the 4th century B.C., it seems to outline an ideal civic order, in which each age-group, from the *puer* to the old *pater familias*, has its role. In the last quarter of the century, eschatological meanings and the wish to portray the deceased as a hero become increasingly evident in Paestan paintings, which gradually lose their characteristic of mass-production, both in the repertory of images and in their stylistic quality.

Often, in the same tomb, each slab becomes an autonomous painting, although, at the same time, the connections between the figures on different slabs indicate a wish to create a unitary narration.

In tomb 58 in Andriuolo, the two short slabs appear as two independent paintings. The splendid rider and the *prothesis* surpass in monumentality and technical quality other mass-produced works, even abolishing the subdivision of the slab. On the other hand, the images on the two long slabs, with their colors and play of shades, their duel scenes and fights between griffins and panthers, although they are drawn with great expertise, do not rise above the limits imposed by the repertory. That the sce-

51

nes on the different slabs are connected, not casually assembled, is proved by the flute player and the two mourning women at the right extremity of the northern slab, whose behavior only makes sense when referred to the *prothesis* on the adjacent slab. In a similar scene in tomb 4/1971 in Andriuolo, the exaggerated gestures of the mourning women, rhythmically underpinned by the flute-player, charge the composition with pathos. A masterful use of color gives depth to this picture, as in the duel scene in the same tomb, in which the opponents, one seen in profile and the other at a three-quarters angle, in the act of drawing his sword, are arranged on different planes according to a centripetal scheme. In this case, the compositional unity of the scenes painted on the slabs is emphasized by the columns and knotted bands drawn at the four corners of the chamber.

Forms of hero worship are more explicitly represented in the semi-chamber tomb 86 in Andriuolo, featuring an allegoric image of a Nike, racing with outstretched wings on a chariot towards an imposing Doric column. This scene appears on both of the long slabs, thus ideally surrounding the rider's triumphal return and a scene featuring a carriage drawn by mules, a probable allusion to the voyage towards the Beyond.

The decoration of tomb 114 in Andriuolo, of the same period, is the product of a workshop that uses more traditional motifs, some directly drawn from the repertory of the first half of the 4th century, others partially renewed with the insertion of new patterns and the development of pictorial research. In the tomb, the image of the deceased appears on both the short slabs, on one side riding with a war trophy, on the other standing beside his steed in a heroic attitude. In both cases, the horse is isolated between two columns, but has a narrative connection with the figures on the long slabs: by reading the scenes in their sequence, according to the orientation of the figures, one realizes that the knight with the trophy is completed by the woman and the *hydrophora* of the right extremity of the south long slab and by the youth drawn at the left end of the north long

*Paestum.
Andriuolo necropolis,
tomb 114. East slab:
rider standing beside
his horse.
330-320 B.C.*

slab who, all together, make up the scene of the return of the warrior. Neither is the heroic rider totally isolated, as he is in connection with the male individual depicted at the left extremity of the southern slab who, as he follows him, makes a gesture apparently half-way between salute and deprecation. The narration of this tomb is completed on the south slab by a compendium of ritual ceremonies and on the north one by a totally new scene with a realistic or possibly even historical content, i.e. a landscape represented by mountains and oxen in which two groups of armed men confront one another. The one on the right is connoted as the winning side, as it is led by an individual displaying heroic nudity, in the act

53

*Paestum. Andriuolo
necropolis, tomb 114.
North slab: battle scene.
330-320 B.C.*

of hurling his spear, probably to be identified with the Italic Mars. All these works herald the creation of the great pictorial decorative programs of the tombs of Spinazzo, the fullest expression of the Paestan Italic community on the eve of the city's Romanization.

THE CITY IN THE 4TH CENTURY B.C.

At the end of V century b.C. the necropolises prove that the city was conquered by the lucanians. Aristoxenos of Tarentum, the philosopher and musicologist, a pupil of Aristotle, in a book on symposium some fragments of which have reached us, comments on the condition of the barbarized Poseidoniates. The passage, which is not devoid of rhetoric overtones, deserves to be read in its entirety:

> *We behave as the Poseidoniates who live on the Tyrrhenian Gulf. It happened that these people passed from their original condition of Greeks to that of barbarians, having become Etruscans or Romans, that they changed their language and other customs and today still celebrate only one Greek feast, having gathered for which they commemorate the ancient names and ancient laws, they pity one another and, after shedding many tears, they leave.*

54

Around 335 B.C., Alexander the Molossus, king of Epirus (and uncle of Alexander the Great), even tried to appeal to Greek "nationalism" against the Samnites. He occupied Paestum and defeated the Samnites and the Lucanians in battle. After his death, a few years later, the previous situation was re-established.

As far as we know (considering that systematic exploration of the city has only recently begun), between the middle of the 5th and the middle of the 4th century B.C. no major innovations are observable in the town area with respect to the preceding period, concluded by the erection of the *ekklesiasterion* and of the temple of Neptune.

It should be kept in mind, however, that the evidence at our disposal only concerns the sanctuaries and the agora, while we are not yet acquainted with the history of the private dwelling quarters, whose exploration has halted at the Roman-age levels.

Within the limits of the information provided by the architecture of the sacred and public spaces, in can be observed that the most important buildings of the preceding periods continue to be used, e.g. the *ekklesiasterion*, which still had a role in the institutional life of the Lucanian city (cf. the stele with a dedication to Jupiter in the following pages). It is only from the middle of the 4th century B.C. that significant building activity is again attested.

Some areas were monumentalized with the erection of great stone porticoes, such as the one bordering the east-west *plateia* (the street going from Porta Marina to Porta Sirena) and the one that was erected in the middle of the agora, which runs perpendicularly to the amphitheater, and was partially rebuilt by Sestieri in the '50s.

The latter was obviously meant to front a row of stores, and is thus a sign of the commercial function of this part of the square, while to the north (where the *ekklesiasterion* and the *heroon* lie) the area maintained its prevalently political function.

Within the urban sanctuary lying to the south, the most important building of this period (end of the 4th century B.C.), there is an enclosure containing a raised dais paved with rock slabs and preceded by a court. It is probably to

Paestum. Porta Marina. Tract of the city wall on the western side. 4th century B.C.

be identified as a sanctuary of Asclepius, the dais being the *abaton*, i.e. the part where one could not enter freely before having performed sacrifices according to a strict ritual.

The sick were healed in the *abaton* through incubation (i.e. in their sleep).

One of the most outstanding public works of this period is the construction of the first phase of the city walls. Their present appearance is the result of numerous Roman-age rebuilding interventions, but the western tract, with its circular towers, goes back to the end of the 4th century B.C.

THE SQUARE BUILDING OF THE HERAION ON THE SELE

A few years after the Lucanian conquest, in the sanctuary of Hera near the bank of the Sele, a monument which has yielded very interesting information on the religious history of this period was erected. Because of its shape (11 x 11 meters), it was called "square building" by Zancani, who excavated it, unearthing two rich votive deposits, one overlying the other. In the most ancient, she brought to light drinking cups, a great black-figure *dinos* and many silver coins were found, as well as other objects. All these finds are datable between the end of the 6th and the middle of the 5th century B.C., except for a lamp supported by four female figures which is more ancient, dating from the beginning of the 6th century B.C. The more recent deposit (dating from ca. 400 B.C. on) contained a marble statuette of Hera enthroned with the pomegranate, and a number of votive objects (nuptial vases, perfume vases, bread moulds, jewellery) alluding to the role of women as guardians of the domestic space and of the wealth of the house. The square building itself was built at the beginning of the 4th century B.C. to contain the marble statue and the

Heraion on the Sele. Marble statuette from the square building. End of the 5th century B.C.

57

offerings of the more recent deposit, but it probably replaced an earlier building to which the more ancient deposit belonged. The more recent deposit also appears to evoke the female world, although in different ways (the presence of vases used to store or drink wine possibly allude to the nuptial sphere).

THE COUNTRYSIDE
Permanent settlement of the countryside is well documented, especially from 360-350 B.C., by several dozens of farms, each the residence of a family possessing and cultivating the land, and living in a rural house always associated with a small necropolis. Towards the end of the 4th century B.C., this phenomenon suddenly declines, possibly as a consequence of the concentration of land ownership in the hands of a few families.

LANGUAGE, INSTITUTIONS AND COINS

Aristoxenos of Tarentum observes that the Poseidoniates "happened, from their previous condition of Greeks, to become barbarians, and to change their language and their other customs, to the point of celebrating only one of the Greek feasts, during which the participants commemorate ancient institutions and, after having cried, leave".
The Poseidoniates' loss of the Greek language and customs was thus, for Aristoxenos, the most evident sign of the loss of Greek identity.
This loss, however, was never total, as the Greek model always maintained its cultural prestige, even from a linguistic point of view, as the continuing use of the Greek language bears out.
Paestan vases still bear Greek inscriptions such as the signature of the ceramographer ("*Assteas egraphen*", "*Python egraphen*", i.e. "Assteas painted", "Python painted"), the name of the characters depicted on the vases, that of the owner of the vase (Dionysios, Philistos, Polyxenos, Alexis, Emauta, Sagon) or, again, cultic

inscriptions mentioning Hera (by her acronym or her full name), Dionysus or Aphrodite in forms and ways already attested in the city during the Greek period. Ancient formulae are still used, e.g. votive dedications such as *"anetheke dekatan"*, i.e. "dedicated as a *decima*" (i.e. a tithe).

The Greek language was also used in the writing of Oscan names, e.g. the name Plasos on one of the painted slabs of tomb 1 from Gaudo. The only inscription written in Oscan, the language spoken by the Samnites

Paestum. Andriuolo necropolis, tomb 11/1969. Fish plate with the inscription "of Dionysus". End of the 4th century B.C.

59

Paestum. Black-painted pottery sherd with the inscription "Hera". Beginning of the III century B.C.

and their descendants (Campanians, Lucanians, Brettii), was found inside the city and dates from the last decades of the Lucanian domination of Paestum, a period of intense monumental building activity. It is a plastered limestone stele found in the *ekklesiasterion*, the gathering place for the public assemblies built during the Greek phase of the city, but also used by the Lucanians. This stele bears a four-line inscription: "Statis ..*ies* to Jupiter ...*anar* erected [in return] for a favor". It is a dedication to Jupiter on the part of an individual named Staiis or Statis, probably a Paestan *meddix* (the highest institutional office), in return for an unspecified favor (*brateis datas*). The remains of a lead cramp on the upper part of the cyma indicate that the stele probably originally supported a bronze statuette of the god. It is noteworthy that the only inscription in Oscan found in Paestum to date refers to an institutional act. From an exclusively linguistic point of view, this inscription shows that the Oscan spoken in Paestum was the same as that of the rest of Campania and Lucania.

Paestan coinage also continued without significant changes with respect to the past, a sign that the political transition did not bring about radical changes in the economical and social structure of the city. Nevertheless, new symbols and initials were introduced, reflecting the change in the organization presiding over the mints.

The images of Greek deities appeared on coins, clearly expressing a wish to stress cultural continuity with the preceding period. Some elements of the most ancient Poseidoniate coins were reintroduced, an allusion to the

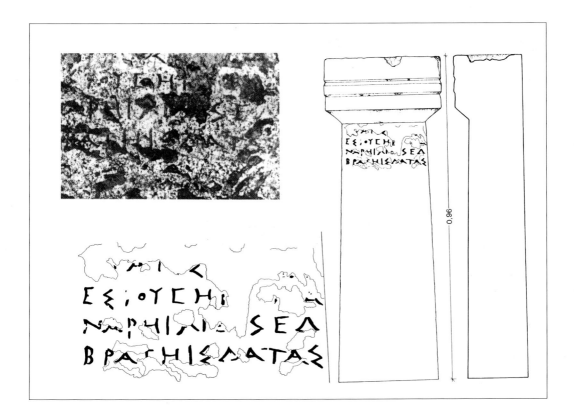

origins of the city. The presence of Poseidoniate coins in the Metapontine, Apulian and Salentine areas is evidence of the close relationship of the Lucanian city with these areas, where Tarentine influence was felt more strongly.

In the course of the 4th century B.C., the Poseidoniate monetary system changed remarkably.

At the middle of the century, new methods of production entailed the abandonment of the use of silver for coins in favor of bronze and an increase in the number of coins produced.

At the end of the century, a new transformation is announced by rare silver staters with the inscriptions PAISTANO, decorated with a male head and a horn identifiable as the personification of the Sele, associated with the Dioscuri on horseback, saluting.

These coinages, clearly inspired by Roman models,

Paestum. From the ekklesiasterion. Stele with Oscan inscription.

61

reflect the ideological and political influence of Romanized Campania on Lucanian aristocracies at the end of the 4th and the beginning of the 3rd century B.C.

THE CULTS OF LUCANIAN PAESTUM

The substantial changes brought about by Lucanian political domination are not as immediately manifest in the religious life of the city as they are in burial customs. On the contrary, the archaeological evidence indicates the continuity of the earlier cults in the urban sacred areas and on the territory.

The topography of the sanctuaries of the city undergoes no modification. There are even traces of restoration carried out on the temples of Athena and Hera immediately after the conquest. It is only in the final decades of the century, when the socio-political structure of Paestan society shows signs of deep change, mainly observable in the necropolis, that new cult buildings appear in the southern sacred area and in the agora, although they do not alter the organization of the *sacra* of the Greek city.

It should be kept in mind that, due to the lack of testimonies in the ancient sources, the majority of the information available on the religion of Paestum in the 4th century B.C. derives from the vast number of votive offerings dedicated by the faithful, the best preserved evidence of the city's cults.

With few exceptions, they consist of moulded terracotta statuettes representing deities or the dedicator himself or, again, food offerings, mainly fruit. They have been found associated with pottery used in the different phases of the offering rituals, and vases with particular forms, connected to the specific functions that Lucanian society assigned to the sexes.

In the southern sanctuary, the unpretentious but innumerable votive objects dated to this period bring further evidence of the persistence of the ancient cult of Hera, which is attested epigraphically until the beginning of the 3rd century B.C. on the bottom of cups on which

Paestum. From the southern urban sanctuary. Hera enthroned. Beginning of the 4th century B.C.

the name of the goddess is painted or incised in Greek alphabet and language, a custom documented for at least two centuries.

The terracotta statuettes represent the goddess enthroned, wearing her royal dress and holding a patera and a fruit-basket, according to an iconography created in the Paestan area in the last decades of the 5th century B.C., and continuing without iconological modifications until the Romanization of the city. Some of the statuettes represent the goddess nursing a baby or holding it

63

Paestum. From the southern urban sanctuary. Hierogamia of Zeus and Hera. 4th century B.C.

under her mantle, emphasizing her function as *kourotrophos*. They were offered as auspices of fertility, or in thanks for a successfully concluded gestation, and reflect the fundamental aspiration to the continuity of the family. This aspect of the adoration of the goddess is already present in the earliest documents of her cult.

The terracotta votive offerings representing scenes of *hierogamia*, featuring the goddess sitting on the throne with her husband Zeus, belong to the same devotional sphere.

They symbolize the divine couple's function, in Greek religion, of guaranteeing legitimate marriage.

The most significant aspects of female life, marriage and reproduction, are thus placed under the protection of the goddess. Further references to the matrimonial sphere are found on bottles bearing painted gynaeceum scenes depicting the bride's toilette.

The scenes decorating nuptial lebes, vases donated by brides, are more rare, but have a similar meaning. They all represent a version of Paris' judgement in which it is Hera who receives the apple designating the most beautiful of the three goddesses, whereas in the traditional version of the myth it is assigned to Aphrodite.

Just as the southernmost part of the urban sanctuary continues to be dominated by Hera, the healing cult practiced in the east-central part of the sacred area, which seems to revolve around the figure of Apollo (to whom it has been recently proposed to attribute the Temple of Neptune) also shows clear signs of functional continuity. The healing properties of the spot are even stressed by the creation of new cultic buildings, if the sanctuary of Asclepius, the divine physician connected to Apollo, in some traditions identified as his son, has been correctly dated.

In the southern temenos, there are also traces of the veneration of Heracles, to whom a cult was possibly dedicated at the northern extremity of the sanctuary. This deified hero is evoked by bronze statuettes representing him in combat and small votive clubs, among the rare votive objects of this period to feature typically Italic iconographies.

This cult, however, is not newly-adopted: the "mythical presence" in Greek Poseidonia is already mentioned by ancient authors and, moreover, the cult of Heracles, closely connected with the figure of Hera, may have had an important role within the religious system of the polis.

The only Greek epigraphic document of the urban cult of Aphrodite is datable between the end of the 4th and the beginning of the following century.

This cult is otherwise attested in Poseidonia only by statuettes of the naked goddess of the 6th century B.C. found in excavations north of the so-called Temple of Neptune. We do not know whether it should be considered an urban duplicate of the far more important cult of Aphrodite practiced in the extra-mural sanctuary of S. Venera, south of the city, where the goddess, the object of intense veneration from the beginning of the 6th century B.C., was given, in the Lucanian period, the epithet of *Iovia*. At the opposite extremity of the city, the cult of Athena is still centered, during Lucanian domination, on the late-Archaic temple of the goddess, as restorations carried out in this period bear out. Its continuity is further stressed by an enormous quantity of fictile statuettes of the goddess, generally depicted wearing a Phrygian-type helmet, the aegis and the shield decorated with the head of the Gorgon. Some of the votive terracottas offered to the goddess represent miniature armor, reflecting

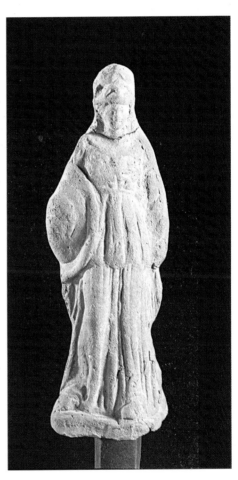

Paestum. From the northern urban sanctuary. Statuette of Athena, standing, with helmet and aegis. 4th century B.C.

65

the Greek tradition of consecrating weapons in sanctuaries, also adopted by the Samnites and the Lucanians.

In the political heart of the city, the agora, which maintained its previous functions, although within a changed political context, the *heroon*-cenotaph of the founder remained the seat of a public cult. The continuity of the cult of Zeus Agoraios, to which a small temple near the *Ekklesiasterion* has been attributed with convincing arguments, is confirmed by the discovery, in the latter building, of a stele written in Oscan and dedicated to Jupiter, the Lucanian transposition of Zeus. This valua-

Heraion on the Sele. Hera Ilitia (assisting childbirth). 4th century B.C.

ble document, so far the only testimony in Paestum of the language of the Lucanians, proves that the *Ekklesiasterion* and the political activity it housed where placed under the divine tutelage of Zeus.

Furthermore, in specifying the name and theological physiognomy of the god, it reveals the degree of awareness with which the elite of the Lucanian city adapted to their own needs the pre-existing cult of Zeus, who had been the protector of this part of the agora since Greek times.

In the religious culture of 4th century Paestum, the most pregnant aspect is continuity with the previous tradition, upheld not only by the now subordinate Greek *ethnos*, but also by the new wielders of political power, who tend to present themselves as continuators of the Greeks.

In the cult centers of the territory, the effects of Lucanian conquest are more evident than in the urban sanctuary. In the Heraion at the mouth of the Sele, the traces of a vast fire are followed by evidence of building activity, the main result of which is the so-called Square Building. The latter contained a marble image of the goddess, whose cult seems, from the nature and type of the remaining material testimonies, to be connected to the functions that Lucanian society assigned to women.

A very remarkable cultural aspect, although less spectacular, is represented by the *sanctua* of the rural sanctuaries. In the best known, the one dedicated to Demeter, in the countryside of Albanella, 13 kilometers north-east of Paestum, there are signs of the persistence of a cult which was centered, from the beginning of the 5th century B.C., on a quadrangular enclosure, under the floor of which vase offerings and the remains of sacrificed piglets were found. The votive material dated to the Lucanian period, prevalently fictile statuettes generally depicting female and male figures with a piglet, confirms that the cult celebrated in the sanctuary was very probably that of Demeter or of a goddess whom the frequenters of the sanctuary identified with her. The ritual actions that have left material traces, apart from the

67

deposition of votive objects, mainly consist of sacrificial meals, prepared and consumed collectively, a custom attested both by the Greek written tradition on the feasts celebrated in honor of the goddess and by the archaeological evidence from other sanctuaries of Demeter.

They prove that the frequenters of the sanctuary consciously conformed to the ritual behavior typical of the tradition of the goddess' cult. A later cult, no earlier than the 4th century B.C., is documented in an area 6 kilometers north-east of Paestum, dominated by Mount Capaccio and near the springs of Capodifiume.

The votive objects, prevalently female busts wearing a high *polos* decorated with rosettes (very similar to specimens from the sanctuary of Demeter in Heraclea), erotes and vase-forms identifiable as cosmetics containers, and hence evoking the female sphere, suggest that the goddess venerated here was possibly Persephone-Kore.

The only evidence of religious beliefs regarding the Beyond in 4th century Paestum is provided by its necropolis.

The adoption of the beliefs, values

68

and mentality of the Greek community in some instances gave rise to funerary customs with specific ritual characteristics, or influenced by currents of religious thought centered on individual salvation after death. An example of the first case is the burial of children and adolescents, i.e. of those members of the community who have not carried out a social function.

They are accompanied by the same statuettes (enthroned goddess and goddess holding a child) offered as votive gifts in the sanctuaries of the city, to compensate them for their premature death and to protect their voyage in the nether world. As to doctrines of salvation after death, they are probably alluded to in the deposition, only observable in the tombs of high-ranking individuals, of eggs, explicit symbols of life and rebirth.

Paestum. Mould for a female head. 4th century B.C.

THE HANDICRAFT

COROPLASTICS (TERRA-COTTAS)

During the Lucanian political rule, the Paestan coroplastic production (i.e. production of figured terracottas) shows total continuity with the preceding period. The models created during the 5th centuries continue to be reproduced with absolute fidelity, although with occasional modifications in style. The Italic characteristics exhibited by the coroplastics of other Lucanian towns are completely missing in the iconography and formal language of the Paestan products. On the backs of the moulds, Greek acronyms and personal names appear, attesting that (regardless of the various different models that have been used to interpret them), just as Paestan pottery painters signed themselves with the Greek names of Assteas and Python, figured objects expressing religious piety were

69

Paestum.
Fictile bust.
4th century B.C.

also produced under the direction of Greek craftsmen. Although we know nothing of the relations between the latter, the means of production and the new rulers, it is certain that, in the 4th century B.C., the coroplastic workshops of Poseidonia reach their climax. No longer working merely to satisfy internal demand, they now export their products in ever increasing quantities to the town centers of Oscan Campania and Lucania. The most common exports include the image, created in the preceding century, of Athena *Promachos* ("about to engage in combat"), specimens of which have been found both in nearby Fratte and in the Irpinian sanctuary of the Mephitis of Ansanto, and the even more diffused statuettes of the enthroned goddess with a *phiale* and a basket containing pomegranates and of male and female offerers with a piglet. Their territorial distribution suggests that these votive offerings, originally conceived for the Greek forms of the cult and, in the case of the ephebi with a piglet, for the cult of Demeter typical of Poseidonia, were used, more than other sacred figures, within several different religious contexts of the Oscan-Lucanian pantheon. The image of the so-called Paestan Hera could very well be used to impersonate other goddesses with royal characteristics, such as the central figure of the domestic and gentile cult of the site of Roccagloriosa, or Mephitis, to whom the sanctuary in the valley of the Ansanto is dedicated. As to the terracottas representing male and female figures with a piglet, found in great numbers, along with the enthroned goddess images, in the sanctuary of Fratte, they may have been connected to the Demeter-type cults, which had such an important role in Italic religion, and may have heralded the conscious adoption by the Italics of central Italy, as early as the 5th century B.C., of votive objects specific to the cult of Demeter.

Other types of votive objects were created, during this period, under the impulse of a persisting and profound acceptance of Greek models and of contacts with Siceliot products, possibly mediated by Neapolis and Tarentum.

The numerous fictile busts used in these Demeter-type cults, documented in the city as early as the late-Archaic period, are inspired by Syracusan and Agrigentine models. They include busts cut under the breast, wearing modeled earrings and necklaces or a high tapering *polos*, and busts lacking modeled applications, cut under the shoulders. The Sicilian image of Artemis, wearing a high-knotted coiffure and *endromides* (pointed shoes), carrying the bow and with a dog on her right, provided the model for the votive objects found in the urban sanctuaries of Poseidonia, especially near the Athenaion.

These terracottas, mainly imitating Syracusan types and others from the hinterland of Gela, are among the few documents suggesting there was an urban cult of Artemis in Poseidonia.

This iconographic theme, like the busts, was reproduced by the Poseidionate craftsmen without substantial modifications with respect to the prototypes.

The version of the iconographic model found in the sanctuary of Mephitis in Ansanto, in the interior of Campania, is of Poseidoniate origin.

Many votive terracottas belonging to the very well-known series of the "recumbents", i.e. figures lying on a *kline* (a bed), have been found in the northern sanctuary. In Poseidonia, the theme of the recumbent seems to have been adopted only in the late 4th century B.C., as parallels with similar types from Metapontine contexts bear out, and is an autonomous elaboration, independent from the better-known Tarentine models.

Unlike the latter, it is not accompanied by other figures, nor does it present - with the exception of the *phiale* - the attributes that give the figure a sacred dimension, such as the characteristic headdress and objects such as the *rhyton* and *kantharos*. The rendering of the facial features stresses

71

the young age of the person depicted. These figures generally present no elements permitting identification with a specific mythological subject.

Their meaning is to be sought within the overall system of coeval offerings from the northern urban sanctuary.

Mention should be made the many hundreds of *thymateria* found in Paestum, depicting female or, more rarely, Silenic busts surmounted by a lily flower, and produced between the 4th and 3rd century B.C.

*Paestum.
"Flower woman" bust.
4th century B.C.*

They provided the model for similar specimens found in Capua, Selinus and Lipari. The female types, better known as "flower-women", have also been interpreted as votive offerings connected to the cult of *Hera Antheia* (Hera "of the Flowers"), *"Antheia"* being an epithet of the goddess in Argos (Paus. II,22,1) as a guardian of female fecundity and of the fertility of the fields. It is more likely, however, that these objects had a less specific value. They were mere perfume-burners (it matters little if they were actually used or not) and, having been found in various contexts, they were probably indifferently used in the cults of more than one deity.

The artistic traditions of early Hellenism, which provided the inspiration for these productions, also stimulated, here as elsewhere, the creation of a countless series of draped female images, generically defined as "tanagrines", which reproduce models common to the entire Hellenized world, from the Mediterranean to the Black Sea.

Most of them represent young women, standing or striding self-assuredly, more rarely sitting down or leaning on a small pillar. Almost all the best and more ancient pieces, still presenting traces of color, have been found in burials.

They document a direct connection with the coroplastic workshops of Tarentum, one of the main Southern Italian centers to adopt and elaborate on the figurative and stylistic language of early Hellenism (Tarentum also had a decisive influence on other and far more significant artistic productions of Poseidonia in this period).

Most of the Paestan tanagrines, also including large-size figures assembled from several separately moulded pieces, a highly specialized technique, are the fruit of very standardized processes of average qualitative level.

As in the previous decades, Paestan terracottas were still diffused outside the strictly local circuit, but were now exported especially to Capua, where the abovementioned "flower-women" have been found, as well as some rare types of "tanagrines", so far attested only in these two cities.

After the thousands of Paestan terracottas from this period are published, it will be possible to provide a clearer picture of the role of the local workshops in the relations between production centers and in the dynamics of the diffusion of models.

Paestum. Sitting female figure. End of the 4th century B.C.

CERAMICS

Along with the traditional productions of unpainted and black-painted vases, Paestan craftsmen, around the end of the 5th century B.C., began to fabricate vases with red figures painted on a background surface completely painted in black, not a very common technique, but attested, in slightly earlier times, both in Greece and in Etruria.

Not much later, in the first decades of the 4th century, a new local production begins.

It consists of vases made according to the most commonly employed method of leaving the surface to be occupied by the decoration unpainted, and painting the rest of the object black. In Paestum, as elsewhere, the beginning of the production of local red-figured pottery is a consequence of the assimilation of various traditions and influences

73

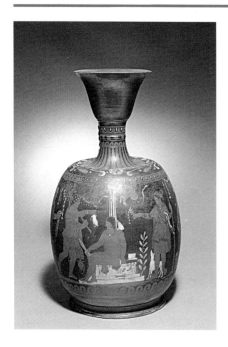

Paestum. Gaudo necropolis, tomb 2/1957. Lekythos made by Assteas, representing the purification of Orestes in Delphi. Middle of the 4th century B.C. ca.

Paestum. Andriuolo necropolis, tomb 24. Neck-amphora signed by Python, depicting the birth of Helen from the egg. 340-330 B.C.

that are not merely juxtaposed, but re-elaborated in an original way, giving rise, before long, to a specific style.

The most representative Paestan ceramist is Assteas, whose name is known from his signature on his most elaborate vases, a custom attested in Attic ceramography of the 5th century, but unusual among Italiots such as the Paestans. The signature of Assteas appears on eleven vases decorated with scenes conceived in a theatrical way, often flanked by two small pillars, and with the decorated space divided into two registers. In the upper register, busts are represented, mainly belonging to deities, while in the lower register the characters are arranged symmetrically on the sides of the main character who is the axis of the representation.

In the most complex scenes, the characters are identified by their names written close to their heads.

The works of Python, the other Paestan ceramist who signed some of his works, are directly derived from the tradition of Assteas and his workshop. Python seems, however, to have been less prolific, as the vases bearing his signature are only two, as compared to Assteas' eleven. Around the middle of the 4th century, numerous other artistic personalities flourished, one of the most conspicuous being the Painter of Aphrodite, so called from the scene painted on the great neck-amphora found in tomb 13 in the locality of Licinella. His style and the use of superimposed white and yellow painting characterize this painter as the most representative exponent of an artistic trend conventionally called "Apulianizing", diffused in this period throughout southern Italy and well attested in Paestum by wall paintings as well as ceramics.

Other vases adhere more closely to Campanian models, e.g. Naples 1778 and 2585, decorated by painters of the late 4th century, a period in which the decline of the Paestan red-figured ware had begun.

LUCANIAN PAESTUM AT THE EVE OF ROMANIZATION

From the end of the 4th century to the foundation of the Latin colony of 273 B.C., the use of funerary paintings was considerably reduced, being reserved exclusively to a few chamber tombs.

Burial equipment also became simpler. In male tombs, the strigil, sometimes associated with a ring, is a commonly featured gravegood, while female tombs contain loom weights, rings and fibulae. In both, the most recurrent pottery types are drinking vases (*skyphoi*), pyxides, cups, bottles, ointment containers and *lekanai*. Child burials contain miniature objects, notably figured terracottas often reproducing theatrical masks and comical misshapen characters of the Fliacic comedy.

Paestum. Gaudo necropolis, tomb 2. Lekane of the "Group of the red and black" with a papposilenus playing a double flute. 340-330 B.C.

The new ideology is more clearly expressed by the tombs of the necropolis of Spinazzo, which extends south of the walls, occupying an area previously only occasionally used for Archaic age burials. In this sector, out of 120 graves, prevalently of the chest and trench type, only 12 are chamber tombs, 7 of which are present a painted decoration on their internal walls. These tombs form a center around which other coeval burials are arranged, possibly reflecting family ties. The paintings celebrate Paestan aristocracy through the exaltation of the genealogy of the deceased. The repertory of the scenes is repetitive, being always centered on the meeting and reciprocal greeting of two characters facing one another, towering on the central wall opposite the entrance room. Each is followed by a cortege weaving its way on the lateral slabs. The figures are life-size, taking up all the height of the chamber, and are contoured with a thin brown line, while their complexion is rendered with strokes of different shades of pink. On the central wall of the most representative tomb of this group, an aged character with white beard and hair holds with his right hand the right hand of a young man facing him. The latter is followed by a youth carrying a

Paestum. Licinella necropolis, tomb 69. Neck-amphora of the Aphrodite Painter, on which the apparition of the goddess is represented. 340-330 B.C.

75

Paestum. Spinazzo necropolis, tomb 4. Skyphoidal pyxis of the Spinazzo Painter. End of the 4th-beginning of the 3rd century B.C.

Paestum. From the ekklesia-sterion. Bottom of a kylix on which a male head wearing a Phrygian beret is depicted. Beginning of the 3rd century B.C.

spear and a shield and holding the reins of a horse painted on a lateral wall, which in its turn is followed by a second steed carrying a load on the top of which is a small dog. These splendid horses, of enormous size, are followed by a young male character, painted on one of the jambs of the entrance door, who brings up the rear of the cortege accompanying the young man on the central wall to his meeting with the aged one. On the other slab, another cortege is painted. It is centered on the triumphal return of a rider who strides toward a matron with veiled head and wearing jewellery, who greets him holding out to him a golden patera. The men wear long white tunics with red-brown borders and decorations, held at the waist by a belt whose yellow color reproduces that of gilded bronze. Their wear high laced boots and splendid crowns.

The faces of the characters of these tombs are different one from the other, and may hence be portraits. The high quality of the paintings bears witness to the level of skill attained by these local artists, who had mastered solutions elaborated by the great contemporary Greek painting such as, for example, the *trompe l'oeil* rendering of the shadows of objects to give the illusion they were hanging from the walls. The decorative program of this tomb makes explicit, through a play of reciprocal allusions between the long slabs and the central scene, the pivot of the entire representation, that the deceased has earned, during his lifetime, the honors and the triumph due to the members of his lineage, and can thus take his place among the ancestors represented by the old *pater familias* who greets him holding out his hand. These paintings show that, at the beginning of the 3rd century B.C., the Paestan aristocracy was deeply Hellenized and, at the same time, had adopted in full, even before it was proclaimed a Latin colony in 273 B.C., the manners and customs of the neighboring Romanized Campanian elites.

Paestum. Necropolis of Spinazzo, tomb. The parting of a young and an old man. Beginning of the 3rd century B.C.

Paestum. Necropolis of Spinazzo, tomb. Procession of horses. Beginning of the 3rd century B.C.

Paestum. Spinazzo necropolis, tomb 1, called "Tomb of the Magistrate". Old bearded man showing his ring. 3rd century B.C.

77

GENERAL BIBLIOGRAPHY

For further reading on the subjects dealt with in this book, we recommend the following bibliography.

In general
E. Greco, I. D'Ambrosio, D. Theodorescu, *A Guide to Poseidonia-Paestum*, Taranto 1995

Poseidonia-Paestum from the foundation to the Lucanian conquest
F. Krauss, *Die griechischen Tempeln*, Berlin 1941
P. Zancani Montuoro, U. Zanotti Bianco, *Heraion alla foce del Sele*, Rome 1951-54
M. Napoli, *La tomba del tuffatore*, Bari 1970
E. Greco, D. Theodorescu, *Poseidonia-Paestum II. L'agorá*, Rome 1983
AA.VV., "Poseidonia-Paestum", *Atti del XXVII Convegno di Studi sulla Magna Grecia, Taranto 1987*, Napoli 1992
D. Mertens, *Der alte Heratempel in Paestum*, Mainz am Rhein 1993

Communities and cultures of southern Campania
A. Pontrandolfo, B. d'Agostino, "Greci, Etruschi e Italici nella Campania e nella Lucania tirrenica", in *Crise et transformation des sociétés archaïques de l'Italie antique au V siècle av. J-C.*, Roma 1990, pp. 101 ff.
AA.VV., *Fratte. Un insediamento etrusco-campano* (G. Greco, A. Pontrandolfo, eds.), Modena 1990.

Samnites and Lucanians from the gulf of Poseidonia to the gulf of Laos (Scalea, Calabria)
F. Prontera , "Sinus ingens Terinaeus", *Annali della facoltà di lettere dell'Università di Perugia* XIII (1975-76), pp. 341-346
AA.VV., "Temesa e il suo territorio", *Atti del Convegno di Perugia, 1981* (G. Maddoli, ed.), Taranto 1982
AA.VV., *A sud di Velia I*, (G. Maddoli, A. Stazio, eds.), Taranto 1990

M. Gualtieri, H. Fracchia, *Roccagloriosa I*, Napoli 1990
AA.VV., *Satriano 1987-88* (E. Greco, ed.), Napoli 1988
AA.VV., *Laos I* (E. Greco, S. Luppino, A. Schnapp, eds.),
Napoli 1989
AA.VV., *Laos II* (E. Greco, P. G. Guzzo, eds.), Napoli 1992
AA.VV., "Laos", *Città e territorio nelle colonie greche d'occi-
dente*, II (E. Greco, D. Gasparri, eds.), Napoli 1995

The Lucanians in Paestum
M. Cipriani, "Nuove ricerche nella necropoli del Gaudo
di Paestum", in *Seminari della fondazione Paestum* (in press)
A. Pontrandolfo, A. Rouveret, *Le tombe dipinte di Paestum*,
Modena 1992
AA.VV., "Paestum", *Città e territorio nelle colonie greche d'oc-
cidente*, I, Napoli 1987
E. Greco, "Edifici quadrati", in *Studi in memoria di Ettore
Lepore* (in press)
A. Ardovino, *I culti di Paestum antica e del suo territorio*,
Salerno 1989
M. Taliercio, "Aspetti e problemi della monetazione di
Poseidonia", *Atti del XXVII Convegno di Studi sulla Magna
Grecia, Taranto 1987*, Napoli 1992, pp. 133 ff.
M. Cipriani, *S. Nicola di Albanella*, Roma 1989
E. Greco, *Il pittore di Afrodite*, Roma 1970
A.D. Trendall, *The Red-Figured Vases from Paestum*,
Roma 1987

CONTENTS